The False Servant

Pierre Carlet de Chamblain de Marivaux (1688–1763) was born into a rich entrepreneurial family in Paris. He lived by investing his ample fortune in foreign markets, writing as a pastime, until he was bankrupted in a financial crash in 1722. Marivaux's style of writing was innovative at the time – so much so that the new style of 'delicate' writing was given his name: 'marivaudage'. *La Fausse Suivante, ou le fourbe puni* was first staged in Paris in 1724. Other plays by Marivaux include *La Double Inconstance*, *La Méprise*, *Les Sincères* and *Les Fausses Confidences*. His novels include *La Vie de Marianne* and *Le Paysan Parvenu*.

Martin Crimp was born in 1956. His plays include *Definitely the Bahamas* (1987), *Dealing with Clair* (1988), *Play with Repeats* (1989), *No One Sees the Video* (1990), *Getting Attention* (1991), *The Treatment* (winner of the 1993 John Whiting Award), *Attempts on Her Life* (1997), *The Country* (2000) and *Face to the Wall* (2002). A short fiction, *Stage Kiss*, was published in 1991 and *Four Imaginary Characters* appeared in 2000 as a preface to *Plays One*. In 2004 the French and German premieres of the short play *Fewer Emergencies* were staged at the Théâtre National de Chaillot and the Schaubühne in Berlin. His previous translation of Marivaux, *The Triumph of Love* (*Le Triomphe de l'Amour*) was staged at the Almeida in 1999, and he has also translated works by Ionesco, Koltès, Genet and Molière.

also by Martin Crimp

MARIVAUX

The False Servant

a new translation by
MARTIN CRIMP

faber and faber

First published in 2004
by Faber and Faber Limited
3 Queen Square, London WC1N 3AU

Typeset by Country Setting, Kingsdown, Kent CT14 8ES
Printed in England by Mackays of Chatham plc, Chatham, Kent

A CIP record for this book
is available from the British Library

0-571-22496-2

2 4 6 8 10 9 7 5 3 1

The False Servant in this new translation by Martin Crimp
was first presented in the Cottesloe auditorium of the
National Theatre, London, on 26 May 2004. The cast
in order of speaking was as follows:

Frontin David Shaw-Parker
Trivelin Adrian Scarborough
The Chevalier Nancy Carroll
Lélio Anthony Calf
Arlequin David Collings
The Countess Charlotte Rampling

Director Jonathan Kent
Designer Paul Brown
Lighting Designer Mark Henderson
Music Jeremy Sams
Sound Designer Rich Walsh
Company Voice Work Patsy Rodenburg

Characters

The Countess

Lélio

The Chevalier

Trivelin
the Chevalier's servant

Arlequin
Lélio's servant

Frontin
another of the Chevalier's servants

Peasants

Dancers

The action takes place outside
the Countess' château, close to a village
outside Paris.

Passages inside brackets (thus)
are marked 'aside' in the original.

A slash / indicates a suggested overlap.

THE FALSE SERVANT

Act One

SCENE ONE

Frontin, Trivelin.

Frontin My God: that looks exactly like Trivelin. Well, well – the man himself. So, my friend – how are you keeping?

Trivelin Marvellously, Frontin, marvellously – still holding on to my two most famous assets: tip-top health and bottomless appetite. But what are you doing here? You're supposed to be running your own small business in Paris. What happened?

Frontin Went bust, basically. What about yourself? How's life been treating 'His Lordship' since we last met?

Trivelin The way it normally treats a man with high hopes and a low income.

Frontin You mean like shit.

Trivelin Exactly. But it has taught me one lesson: don't tempt fate – don't even attempt to tempt fate. The lower your horizons, the less you can be humiliated – maybe that's all a human being can realistically ask. I'm not happy – but I'm quite happy not to be – that's my philosophy.

Frontin Christ, you've always been one step ahead of the game – but for a man like yourself to renounce worldly goods – to take up philosophy – well, I'm impressed.

Trivelin No – wait – stop – this is embarrassing – nobody said 'renounce'. My disdain, such as it is, for worldly goods is probably so much bullshit. And

3

between you and me, anyone who leaves their valuables in the care of my philosophy leaves their valuables in the care of my philosophy entirely at their own risk. Because deep down, man is a cunt.

Frontin A statement I could not in all conscience contradict.

Trivelin And I can say that to you, Frontin, because I know we speak the same language.

Frontin So – anyway – what's this bundle you're carrying?

Trivelin This bundle, as you call it, depressingly contains everything I own.

Frontin At least you travel light.

Trivelin I've been travelling light for the past fifteen years. You know how hard I've tried – you know I've sweated blood to find some kind of security in this world. I was advised not to have scruples – and it's advice I've scrupulously followed. I've been the perfect gentleman if required – and – against my better judgement – the equally perfect hypocrite. Occasionally I've made money – but money has a habit of disappearing – especially when wine and women are involved – which they invariably have been.

Frontin Absolutely.

Trivelin What can I say? Master on Monday, servant on Tuesday, cautious on Wednesday, cunning on Thursday, aims high Friday, falls low Saturday, crawls back Sunday, starts again Monday. Bowed and scraped to as Mister X, kicked in the teeth as Mister Y – different names, different jobs, different clothes, different personalities – high-risk, low-success-rate – outwardly decent, inwardly debauched – denounced by some, mistrusted by others – basically a totally unknown quantity – except for my

4

debts – which are numerous. I owe money to two kinds of people: the ones who expect it back, and the ones who don't even realise I've taken it. I've slept between clean sheets, infested sheets, bourgeois and aristocratic sheets, out on the streets, and frequently as a guest of the prison service – although I've tried to keep my depressing stays there to a minimum. And basically, my friend, after fifteen years of effort, agony and grief, this pathetic bundle is all I possess – after all my attempts to please, this is what the world's left me: one small pile of crap.

Frontin You're taking it too seriously – although of course no one wants to be a guest of the prison service – so let's move swiftly on. I may have a job for you – although it will rather depend on what you've been up to for the past couple of years.

Trivelin Well, the first thing I did since you last saw me was I signed up.

Frontin What? For the army? You don't mean you've deserted?

Trivelin Not for the army – for domestic service.

Frontin Very good.

Trivelin But before taking this humiliating step, I sold my entire wardrobe.

Frontin You? A wardrobe?

Trivelin Yes – three or four nice little second-hand numbers whose approximate fit had allowed me to pass as a gentleman. I didn't want anything reminding me of my former glory. I was ruthless: sold every last stitch – not only that: drank every last penny.

Frontin Very good.

Trivelin Succeeded, my friend, over a number of degenerate evenings, in committing myself to a life of ongoing poverty – an idea, as it seemed at the time, of sheer alcoholic genius. Until one fine morning, there I was – completely broke. I needed help fast, so a friend of mine suggested I meet this Monsieur So-and-so, a married man in need of a servant, who was an authority on dead languages. This was fine by me – I can handle authority – so I moved in. All he ever talked about was books – the man was obsessed with what he called the 'classics' and totally detested something called 'modernity'. So I asked what he meant.

Frontin And?

Trivelin Well 'classic' – let me get this right – classic is when a writer's extremely old and preferably dead. For example, it could be . . . Homer.

Frontin Could be what?

Trivelin Homer – the poet – we're talking ancient Greek.

Frontin I thought we were talking French.

Trivelin We are talking French (well, trying to), but he was talking ancient Greek – heroes, myths – you know the kind of thing: Helen of Troy, Dido of Carthage, Plaster of Paris. I could go on.

Frontin Never heard of them.

Trivelin Never heard of them? Key figures, my friend, of western civilisation.

Frontin If you say so. So what's 'modernity'?

Trivelin Modernity is . . . well, you, basically.

Frontin Oh? Are you sure about that?

Trivelin Absolutely. You are not just modern, you are ultra-modern. Only a tiny tiny baby is more modern than you and me.

Frontin So what did your employer have against us?

Trivelin Simply the fact that we are not – whatever – four thousand years old. So to ingratiate myself, I learned the names of all these dead authors: Thucydides, Sophocles, Euripides, Simonides, Socrates, Aristophanes, Demosthenes . . . and he was so impressed he let me have a key to the cellar where he kept a particular vintage wine he assured me was 'a classic'. He'd give me the occasional glass – and out of respect for Sophocles and so on, I helped myself to the occasional bottle. Not that I neglected modernity. His wife was much more progressive – so it was in her honour that I tasted the more contemporary wines – and siphoned some off for personal consumption – albeit discreetly.

Frontin I can imagine.

Trivelin Now wouldn't you 've said this would keep them both happy? On the contrary. Instead of appreciating my extreme open-mindedness they called me a thief and threw me out. Was I wrong?

Frontin I'd say you were entirely human. But look: down to business. I'm being sent tonight back to Paris, and while I'm away I need someone to take over from me here and look after my master. Interested?

Trivelin Absolutely. What's he like? Generous with the food? Because for me right now, eating is a priority.

Frontin Very generous – she's a real delight – a great person . . .

Trivelin 'She's a real delight?'

Frontin Mmm?

Trivelin I thought it was a man. What d'you mean, 'She's a real delight'? Is something going on, Frontin?

Frontin Well, yes it is, Trivelin. It isn't a man, it's a girl dressed like one. You weren't meant to know that – but now – well – like an idiot I've told you. Please be discreet.

Trivelin I was born discreet, my friend. So basically you and this girl are plotting something – would that be correct?

Frontin Yes. (But let's not tell him just how important this 'girl' really is . . .) That's her now – back off a bit so I can talk to her.

Trivelin backs off and moves away.

SCENE TWO

The Chevalier, Frontin.

Chevalier Well? Have you found me a servant?

Frontin Yes, Mademoiselle: he's just / waiting to –

Chevalier I've told you not to call me that. The word is 'Monsieur'.

Frontin I'm so sorry, Mademoiselle . . . I mean Monsieur. I've just met a friend of mine – extremely reliable – unexpectedly available due to the sudden death of his previous employer, and very keen to be introduced.

Chevalier I assume you haven't been stupid enough to tell him who I am?

Frontin Please – Monsieur – I do know how to keep a secret (well, at least in theory . . .) Shall I ask him to come over?

Chevalier Of course – then please leave immediately for Paris.

Frontin I'm just waiting for your letters.

Chevalier I don't think letters are a good idea. Someone else might get to read them – and I mustn't have my plans made public. So listen carefully to what I want you to say. You're to tell my sister she's not to worry – but that when some friends took me to a ball disguised like this – like a man – I happened to meet a gentleman I'd never seen before – who I'd been told was out of town – but who turned out to be Lélio – the same Lélio that my sister's husband has been angling for me to marry. Tell my sister that, surprised at finding this man in Paris – where he was not supposed to be – and what's more with a woman, I decided I'd use my disguise to make him open up to me. Tell her I made friends with him incredibly easily, in a man-to-man sort of a way, and that he asked me to join him the following day at the country house of the woman he was with. Explain that that's where we are now and that I've already found out a number of things I need to follow up before I can commit myself to actually marry. Tell her this is extremely important to me. Fetch me this servant of yours, then go immediately back to Paris.

SCENE THREE

The Chevalier (alone).

Chevalier No one owns me, or controls me, and the moment I met Lélio was a gift from God, which I intend to fully exploit. My sister won't be surprised: she knows I'm not scared to be perverse. I have money, yes – but also the capacity to love. These are both great gifts – and I need to know who I'm giving them to.

SCENE FOUR

Chevalier, Trivelin, Frontin.

Frontin (*to Chevalier*) This is the man, Monsieur. (*under his breath, to Trivelin*) Keep the secret to yourself.

Trivelin My lips are as sealed as yours were.

SCENE FIVE

Chevalier, Trivelin.

Chevalier Come over here. What do I call you?

Trivelin Whatever you like, Monsieur – butler on Monday, footman come Tuesday – by the end of the week your unquestioningly faithful slave.

Chevalier Very good – I'm just asking for your name.

Trivelin The fact is is that's a slightly painful request because I'm the first member of my family to serve rather than to be served. Although I do have to say that a man in my position can think of a number of very interesting ways of serving a man like yourself.

Chevalier (What's that supposed to mean? What's he talking about: / interesting ways?)

Trivelin Which is why – Monsieur – it gives me great pleasure to say that my name is Trivelin – a name handed down from father to son as legitimately as is biologically possible – and that from that long line of Trivelins, this one, at this moment, is, thanks to you, the happiest Trivelin of all.

Chevalier I don't need your flattery. All a servant has to do is work.

Trivelin Servant! That's a hard word, which I personally find offensive. Shouldn't this degrading terminology be banned?

Chevalier You're unusually sensitive.

Trivelin Exactly – so let's try and come up with something slightly more intimate, shall we?

Chevalier (This is a joke.) Why are you smiling like that?

Trivelin Simply at the delightful prospect of placing my own humble body entirely at the service of your own.

Chevalier Any more of this and you're dismissed: your behaviour is inappropriate.

Trivelin Inappropriate? I'm sorry, but I don't think that's true.

Chevalier (This is outrageous.) I want you to leave.

Trivelin I'm not going anywhere until you accept that my behaviour is more appropriate than you're prepared to admit.

Chevalier I'm telling you to leave.

Trivelin And I'm telling you I won't.

Chevalier Oh, really?

Trivelin Yes, really – let's stop wasting time and both get down to business.

Chevalier You realise you're playing a very dangerous game?

Trivelin Not dangerous for me: I've nothing to lose.

Chevalier (This idiot's ruining everything.) (*He makes as if to go.*) I'm going. (*to Trivelin*) Are you following me?

Trivelin Of course. I'm not someone who gives up without a struggle. In fact I quite enjoy it.

Chevalier How dare you be so insolent!

Trivelin How can you be so cruel!

Chevalier So *what*?

Trivelin Cruel – that's right – you heard what I said. Well, go on – don't stop – break my heart if it makes you happy.

Chevalier (This is not the conversation I expected.)

Trivelin (That's right – you just think about it – pause to reflect – be more accommodating – and the two of us should reach a healthy compromise – I can picture it now.) My desire to serve you is absolute – it burns in my blood with an unquenchable fire.

Chevalier I shall deal with you in the way you deserve.

Trivelin Please! No violence – that's not your area of expertise. A woman stops a man's heart simply with a glance.

Chevalier I've been betrayed!

Trivelin Game's up, sweetheart – I know who you are.

Chevalier What?

Trivelin Frontin let slip.

Chevalier You mean that idiot told you who I am?

Trivelin All he said was you were female – I don't quibble when it comes to sex.

Chevalier In which case, you might as well hear the rest.

Trivelin Why you're dressed as a man, for example.

Chevalier Not to cause trouble.

Trivelin Obviously – dressed as a woman you'd be more dangerous still.

Chevalier (I'll have to lie.) Look, I was only trying to keep this secret to protect my mistress, a very important person. I'm just a servant – but my mistress – who is keen to marry a man called Lélio – wants me to break up this Lélio's relationship with the Countess who owns this château.

Trivelin What? By getting you to seduce him? Sounds rather high-risk, my sweet and obedient servant.

Chevalier Absolutely not. My job, in this disguise, is to work on the feelings of the Countess. As you can see, I can pass myself off as a fairly attractive young man – and I've already caught her looking my way. If I can make her fall in love with me, I'll force her to break with Lélio: Lélio will go back to Paris – in Paris he'll meet my mistress – and once he's met my mistress – a highly desirable woman – he's sure to marry her instead.

Trivelin And what about us?

Chevalier Us?

Trivelin Are you in a relationship?

Chevalier No.

Trivelin Neither am I. So we already have a great deal in common – wouldn't you say?

Chevalier Possibly.

Trivelin Which is already the basis of a firm friendship – would you agree?

Chevalier All right.

Trivelin Which implies – by the same logic – a degree of friendly give and take: meaning, in return for my total discretion you give me two months' salary in advance. Help behind the scenes will be provided at no additional cost – all I ask for is love.

Chevalier (*giving him money*) Listen, this is three hundred francs for your discretion, and two hundred more for your help.

Trivelin (*with apparent indifference*) That really is two hundred francs too many – but – well – seeing it's you, I'll swallow my pride.

Chevalier Look: that's Lélio. Leave us, and wait for me by the château gates.

Trivelin Now, now – easy does it. I may be your servant in the theatre, but in real life, sweetheart, you are my sex-slave. Just you remember.

He moves back, as Lélio enters with Arlequin. The two servants greet each other.

SCENE SIX

Lélio, Chevalier, Arlequin, Trivelin (behind their masters).

Lélio is lost in thought.

Chevalier He seems to have a great deal on his mind.

Arlequin (*to Trivelin behind them*) Looks to me like you're a drinking man.

Trivelin I am indeed a drinking man – that's very perceptive.

Lélio (*turns towards Arlequin, and notices Chevalier*) Arlequin? Ah – Chevalier – I've been looking for you.

Chevalier What's wrong, Lélio? You seem terribly preoccupied.

Lélio I'll explain. (*to Arlequin*) Arlequin: remind those musicians they're supposed to be setting up for the wedding.

Arlequin Yes, Monsieur. (*to Trivelin*) Time for a quick one, my friend?

Trivelin I never refuse a friend – and I never say no to a drink.

SCENE SEVEN

Lélio, Chevalier.

Chevalier So – listen – what is it? What's wrong? Just say if I can be useful.

Lélio You can be very useful.

Chevalier Go on.

Lélio Are you a true friend?

Chevalier If you feel the need to ask, then clearly not.

Lélio Not so angry – please – point taken. Forget that question – let's move on to the next.

Chevalier Which is?

Lélio Do you play by the rules?

Chevalier Depends what the rules are.

Lélio Music to my ears. So you're not one of these sensitive souls who lets every little thing nag nag nag at his conscience.

Chevalier (This doesn't sound promising.)

Lélio For instance: if a man needs to dump some girl and behaves a bit badly, does that make him any less of a gentleman?

Chevalier What? Just for upsetting a woman?

Lélio Basically.

Chevalier By deceiving her.

Lélio That's basically it.

Chevalier I thought you must be planning rape and pillage at the very least. Please – surely – betraying a woman is what makes a man a man.

Lélio (*pleased*) Exactly. And given that philosophy, you may like to know you're looking at a man who's more of a man than most.

Chevalier (*shocked, but as if charmed*) Oh, really? Well what a pleasure to meet – what a thrill to contemplate a man so honourably dishonest: a traitor understandably proud of his dazzling betrayals.

Lélio (*laughing*) I'm delighted you see it that way. (*Offers his hand: they shake.*) But come on: you look like a bit of a heart-breaker yourself. How many reputations have you left lie bleeding? How many damsels have you distressed? Eh?

Chevalier None – forgive me – all my relationships have been quite ordinary. And unfortunately I only ever seem to meet very sensible women.

Lélio Sensible women? What stone were they lurking under? Must've been some pretty rare specimens. And let's face it: what do these women get out of being so sensible? Absolutely nothing. If a man gets lucky with a girl, he tells the world – and if he doesn't, he pretends he did – either way she loses. Although I have to say I've got lucky more often than I've had to pretend.

Chevalier I find your insouciance captivating.

Lélio But back to business. I'll give you the full break-down of my bad behaviour some other time. You're a youngest son, and consequently none too rich.

Chevalier Correct.

Lélio You're bright and good-looking – can't you guess how we might exploit these assets of yours? What would you say to making a great deal of money?

Chevalier I would naturally say yes – then ask what great deal of money you're talking about.

Lélio What I'm talking about is you and the Countess: get the Countess to fall in love with you, then marry her money.

Chevalier You're joking: you're in love with the Countess yourself.

Lélio Correction: was in love with her – but no longer find it expedient to be so.

Chevalier What? You mean you can switch love on and off like a machine? Tell it to stop – and it just stops? What about the way you feel inside?

Lélio When it comes to love, I feel what I choose to feel. The Countess is attractive: I chose to be attracted. The Countess is rich: I chose to propose marriage. However, recently, down on my estate, someone mentioned this girl from Paris I'd never heard of, who comes complete with twelve hundred thousand a year – whereas the Countess only comes with six. I rapidly calculated that six is less than twelve. And how could my 'love' for the Countess be expected to survive such a persuasive calculation?

It would've been ridiculous – six can't compete with twelve – well, can it? (*Slight pause.*) You look confused.

Chevalier Just confused to hear you question your own arithmetic. Anyone who can add up would see you're right.

Lélio Exactly.

Chevalier So what's the problem? Why should dropping the Countess be an issue? Just do it – find her – show her your calculations – tell her: 'Here are the figures, see for yourself.' Simple. Yes yes: she'll cry, she'll curse arithmetic, she'll call you mercenary, insensitive – which might give a lesser man pause. But a true gentleman like yourself – free as you say of a nagging conscience – listens, smiles, expresses polite regret, and oh so respectfully reverses out of the situation, knowing how proud a man should be, in cases like these, to have been labelled 'liar' or 'hypocrite'.

Lélio Christ – I've been labelled plenty of things – and I've no problem reversing out of a tight corner. I'd've dropped the Countess already if the manoeuvre was simply a social one – but there's one small snag – which is, that to complete the purchase some time ago of a new property, the Countess lent me ten million francs, putting me in her debt.

Chevalier I see – well that's rather different. It's altogether harder to manoeuvre one's way out of a debt – 'defaulter' is not a nice label – broken hearts only lead to reproaches, but bad debts lead to lawyers – if you default, there's nothing I can do.

Lélio Oh, but there is. Because besides the ten million, prior to the loan, the Countess and myself had also drawn up a contract for the same amount, committing us both to the marriage. If it's me who breaks it off, I'll owe for the loan plus the forfeit on the contract, and I don't wish to pay either. Not only that, but she's expecting the ceremony to take place as soon as her brother arrives – which could be any moment. See what I'm saying?

Chevalier (The perfect gentleman.) I think I understand. It goes like this: if I can persuade the Countess to fall in love with me, you think she'd rather pay the forfeit – which would write off your debt of ten million – than go through with this marriage – meaning basically you'll get ten million francs out of her – am I right?

Lélio That is – in essence – the plan.

Chevalier Well it's a very ingenious and lucrative one, a stunning example of what you call your 'bad behaviour'. And let's face it: the honour you've done the Countess, just by proposing to her, is worth ten million all on its own.

Lélio Not a view she'd necessarily share.

Chevalier But d'you think I'll find her receptive – emotionally?

Lélio I'm sure you will.

Chevalier (I'm sure I will, too.)

Lélio I've seen how she enjoys your company – she likes you, you amuse her – just build on that.

Chevalier It's not exactly the kind of marriage I had in mind.

Lélio Why not?

Chevalier Various reasons . . . For one thing, I couldn't in all honesty satisfy her need for love. If she just wanted my friendship, that would be different.

Lélio Come on – who said anything about honesty? Why should a man be forced to love his wife? If you don't love her – too bad – that's her problem, not yours.

Chevalier Of course – just I thought a man ought to love his wife, if only to avoid unpleasant scenes.

Lélio Avoid them? A few unpleasant scenes give you an excuse not to see her – already a huge advantage.

Chevalier Well, in that case, I'm happy to help you. And if I do marry the Countess, my good friend Lélio here can show me how to treat a wife with all due contempt.

Lélio I'll set a bracing example, believe you me. For instance, this girl in Paris, how long d'you think love's likely to last there? A fortnight at the most, then I'll be sick of the sight of her.

Chevalier At least give the poor woman a month – seeing she comes with twelve hundred thousand a year.

Lélio
'There is no art
Can overrule the dictates of the heart.'

Chevalier Did they say she was pretty?

Lélio I've been told she's beautiful – but quite frankly, what the hell? However she starts out, any wife of mine will end up ugly by definition.

Chevalier But look: what if she rebels?

Lélio If she rebels, I have a splendidly isolated property in the country where 'Madame' can take early retirement.

Chevalier Retirement – excellent – sounds ideal. Isolation's good for the soul – nice and melancholy – sad but sweet – all those quiet rural pursuits: she'll be spoilt for choice.

Lélio She can run the place.

Chevalier A charming solution. But look: there's the Countess. One piece of advice: keep pretending you love her. If you seem to lose interest, it'll offend her vanity: she'll chase after you, and I won't stand a chance.

Lélio Don't you worry: I know how to deal with women.

He goes to meet the Countess, who has not yet appeared.

SCENE EIGHT

Chevalier.

Chevalier If I'd married that man he'd've buried me alive. Give him twelve hundred thousand francs a year to be packed off to the country? I'm sorry, Monsieur Lélio, but the cost is too high – and I can do better for myself than that. But since I've got this far, why not go further? Why not try and seduce the Countess, save her from Lélio – and teach the man a lesson.

SCENE NINE

Countess, Lélio, Chevalier.

Lélio (*to the Countess, as he enters*) Those musicians still haven't come, Madame, so I need to find out what's happening. I'll leave you with the Chevalier. He's talking about going – says he feels uncomfortable here with you – doesn't quite trust himself. Which is perfectly understandable, but hardly a cause for concern, as I'm sure you'd agree. The fact is, he's my friend, and if he does have feelings for you, that's hardly going to destroy our friendship. Please make him see sense. I'll be straight back.

SCENE TEN

Countess, Chevalier.

Countess I'm sorry? You didn't really need to make up such a silly excuse to leave, did you? Why not just tell us the real reason you want to go back to Paris?

Chevalier The real reason, Countess, is the one Lélio just gave you.

Countess What? This ridiculous fear of falling in love with me?

Chevalier Fear? It's far more than a fear. Because the damage, Madame, has already been done.

Countess (*laughs*) You poor love-sick boy – I had no idea I was so dangerous.

Chevalier Of course you are: isn't that what your mirror constantly reminds you? Didn't it warn you that if you invited me here one glance from those eyes would violate every rule of hospitality?

Countess My mirror does me no favours, Chevalier.

Chevalier Exactly. How could it? Not when nature itself has already favoured you with perfection.

Countess I really don't see it that way.

Chevalier That's because you see things as a woman – but if you saw them the way I do – and I'm speaking now very much as a man – no compliment could be too extreme.

Countess (*laughs*) You really are the most terrible flirt.

Chevalier I'm not flirting with you, Countess. I don't play games, believe me.

Countess I still think you should hurry back to your little sweetheart or whatever she is in Paris. You're bored here, that's all – and deep down, indifferent.

Chevalier I have no sweetheart in Paris, unless that sweet heart is your own. (*Takes her hand.*) As for indifference, Countess, please please teach it me – if only you could! But it's not within your power, since the only thing you can teach a man is love – it's your one great gift.

Countess I think not, Chevalier.

SCENE ELEVEN

Countess, Chevalier, Lélio, etc.

Lélio Still no sign of our musicians, Madame.

  A commotion. Arlequin and Trivelin appear, drunk.

Although I think we're about to be unavoidably entertained . . .

SONG: TOM AND MARIE

Said bright young Tom to young Marie
Hello Marie, Marie it's me,
You see those leafy trees, Marie
Let's rest a while from work so we
Can find out in that secret glade
How love is made.

Said young Marie to bright young Tom
Oh yes I'd like to come along
I've heard that love is like a song
And like a song goes on and on
But Tom before we start to sing
There's just one thing.

Before I pass one single tree
You first young Tom must marry me
And ask my parents to agree
And ask a clerk and pay the fee
And ask a priest to ring the bell
Or burn in hell.

Said Tom, Marie the tree will pay
The fee and all the leaves will pray
And acorns ring like bells all day
We don't need priests or clerks to say
Who can or can't enter the glade
Where love is made.

So both went in to sing the song
Tom and Marie, Marie and Tom
Sang on and on and on and on
Sang on all day and all night long
Then slept and when the morning came
Began again
Then slept and when the morning came
Began again.

Act Two

SCENE ONE

Trivelin (alone).

Trivelin So here I am playing a minor part as it were in a delightful comedy which also appears quite profitable, paying money upfront plus girl. Of course I could just keep my head down and wait for the happy ending – but can a man of my abilities really be expected not to use them? Isn't there something I could do to help my sex-slave servant achieve her aims? If I were to tell our friend Lélio, say, that the Countess was already falling for 'the Chevalier', he'd get the message much sooner and go back to Paris – where this other woman is waiting for him. I've already hinted that the two of us should have a conversation – but this is him now with the Countess. I'll grab him when they've finished.

SCENE TWO

Lélio, Countess. They enter as if in mid-conversation.

Countess No, Monsieur, I do *not* understand. You make friends with the Chevalier, bring him to my house, then expect me to be deliberately rude – where is the sense in that? You're the one who said how attractive and entertaining he was – and the fact is is I find myself forced to agree.

Lélio (*picks up the word*) Forced? Oh really? I don't know what to say: the word 'forced' seems an unfortunate choice for a woman.

Countess Well, unfortunately I chose it.

Lélio I don't think that's funny.

Countess And why shouldn't a woman be 'forced'? Isn't it good French? Is it grammatically incorrect?

Lélio Of course not: but it reveals a little too much enthusiasm for the merits of the Chevalier.

Countess Oh, does it? Well then, it's guilty as charged. And surely you'll admit it does no harm to savour a man's merits, when those merits are real ones – which is all I meant when I said forced.

Lélio Excuse me – 'savour' is wrong – 'savour' is going too far – the normal word is 'appreciate'.

Countess Look, why don't I just keep my mouth shut till you've given me a list of approved vocabulary? I can see that's the only way I'll get permission to speak.

Lélio Madame – please – indulge my love.

Countess In which case you can indulge my ignorance and explain to me the difference between appreciating and savouring.

Lélio Savouring, Madame, suggests, frankly, that you and the Chevalier are emotionally involved.

Countess Well, I find you emotionally un-involved. You're cold, humourless, and – frankly – increasingly unattractive.

Lélio (Excellent – she'll break the contract.)

Countess I suggest we stop. I'm being crude – and you're no better – it doesn't make for amusing conversation.

Lélio What – and go running back to the Chevalier?

Countess Lélio: can I give you a lesson now? There are moments when you would not be missed here – understood?

Lélio Am I really so unbearable?

Countess Don't make me answer that – you'd only start criticising my choice of words – I know that for a fact.

Lélio And I know for a fact that if you weren't so afraid of coming to the point, you'd make it quite clear that you detested me.

Countess I'll certainly make that clear if this carries on – which it apparently will.

Lélio That seems to be your desire.

Countess My desire? I'm not sure that's something you'd be able to satisfy.

Lélio (*seeming angry and abrupt*) I'm very disappointed in you, Madame.

Countess And if, Monsieur, I do fail to come – to the point – whose fault is that? (*She makes to go.*)

Lélio Stop, Countess. I don't think the pleasure has been so entirely one-sided.

Countess I really don't want to hear this.

Lélio And there is the small matter of the contract . . .

Countess (*angry*) Bothers you, does it? Then break it off. Why not just say that in the first place? Why spend all this time prevaricating?

Lélio Break it off? I'd rather die. It commits you to marry me.

Countess What use is my commitment without my love?

Lélio I'd hoped to have both.

Countess Then why go on insulting me?

Lélio Insulting you? How?

Countess By being jealous for one thing.

Lélio But Jesus Christ! When a man's in love . . .

Countess Please! Control yourself!

Lélio . . . how can he not be jealous? You used to accuse me of not being jealous enough – you said I was too tolerant. Now I'm concerned, you say I'm insulting you.

Countess Oh yes, Monsieur, that's right: I'm completely shallow – isn't that what you're trying to say? A compliment entirely in keeping with the last half-hour's diatribe. And you don't think that's insulting me? I find that extraordinary.

Lélio I did not call you shallow, Madame – I simply pointed out that you used to want me to be jealous. Now that I am, perhaps you'd like to calm down a little and explain why that should pose such a problem.

Countess Calm down? Meaning what – that I'm hysterical?

Lélio Please – just answer my question.

Countess No, Monsieur: no woman has ever been spoken to the way you've just spoken to me – and you're the only man I've ever met who apparently finds me so ridiculous.

Lélio (*looks around*) I'm curious to know who you're talking to, Madame, since it can hardly be to me.

Countess Oh very good: now I'm hallucinating, am I? Do go on, Monsieur, do go on. You don't want to break the contract – but I don't want the 'commitment' – isn't that what you're saying?

Lélio All this effort just to avoid answering a very simple question.

Countess I do not *believe* this: shallow, ridiculous, hysterical, and now I'm evasive – a very flattering portrait. I had no idea, Monsieur, I had no idea what you were really like. Jealousy I can forgive – but your kind is unbearable: a horrible, vicious jealousy, deep-rooted in your personality, symptom of a twisted mind. It's not about being sensitive: it's sheer bad-temperedness, and clearly innate. Don't you see: that's not the kind of jealousy I asked you for – what I wanted was the gentle concern which is the product of a man's modesty and finer feelings, the result of his own self-doubt. A man who feels that way, Monsieur, does not abuse the woman he loves – does not find her ridiculous or evasive or hysterical. His only fear is of no longer being loved – for the simple reason he considers himself unworthy to be so. But that's not something you'd ever understand – your soul lacks that capacity. Jealousy for you is an act of aggression – or simply an act, full stop. You're unreasonably suspicious, you have no respect, no pride, no humility. You pin your hopes on a contract, base a whole relationship on instruments of the law. Contracts, Monsieur Lélio, contracts and suspicion. Is that what you call love? Because I call your love terrifying. Goodbye.

Lélio One last word. You're angry, but you'll be back, because there's a part of you that still respects me.

Countess Oh, absolutely. But you're not the only man to find himself in that position – nor, I have to say, is that position a particularly attractive one to be in.

Lélio To make peace, do me one favour. You are still dear to me – and the Chevalier's in love with you – please be a little less receptive – delicately suggest that he might like to leave us alone together and go back to Paris.

Countess 'Delicately suggest?' You mean casually invent some lie from which he will casually infer I am socially incompetent? I'm sorry, Monsieur, but that isn't something I'm prepared to do. No amount of being delicate can prevent a ridiculous suggestion from looking ridiculous – as your own ridiculous suggestion so clearly and so indelicately proves.

She goes.

SCENE THREE

Lélio, Trivelin.

Lélio (*alone for a moment, laughing*) Excellent, excellent, things are really progressing – I'll get to marry the twelve-hundred thousand. But here's the Chevalier's servant. (*to Trivelin*) You appeared to have something to say to me.

Trivelin Yes, Monsieur – if you'll pardon the liberty. I know the way I'm dressed counts against me – but I do, nevertheless, have the feelings of a gentleman, including a gentleman's natural predilection for money and property.

Lélio I've no doubt.

Trivelin What's more – and I simply mention it – but what's more there was a time when I had money and property myself. But you will know, Monsieur, how unpredictable our lives are. Fate's made a fool of me – but it's not just me Fate's made a fool of: history's one long catalogue of jokes in bad taste. Princes, heroes: Fate crushed them all – and my one consolation is to number myself among them.

Lélio Cut the philosophy and get to the point.

Trivelin The wretched of this earth have a habit of rambling on, Monsieur, naturally inclining towards self-pity. But let me stop there, now this little introduction has – well, hopefully – enhanced my value, and lent some weight to what I'm about to say.

Lélio Which is?

Trivelin You know I'm acting as servant to Monsieur le Chevalier.

Lélio Yes.

Trivelin I can't go on doing it – his lack of conscience leaves mine in a state of shock.

Lélio Oh really? What's he done wrong?

Trivelin You're not like him at all. The moment I saw you, the moment I heard you speak, I said to myself, 'What an honest soul, what a scrupulous individual.'

Lélio I'm sure – but we're wasting time.

Trivelin Monsieur, virtue is always worth digressing for.

Lélio But now to the point.

Trivelin Absolutely – only first can we be clear about one small thing?

Lélio Go on.

Trivelin I'm proud – but I'm poor: two qualities which, as I'm sure you're aware, although hard to reconcile, have a habit of living in close proximity – hence my dilemma.

31

Lélio What dilemma? Where's all this pride and poverty of yours leading us?

Trivelin They're leading us, Monsieur, to the scene of a battle: pride puts up a marvellous defence, but her enemy goes in hard. Pride's soon wounded, pride retreats – deserts – leaves the field to poverty who, in her typically shameless way, appeals to your bank account even as we speak.

Lélio You mean you want money in return for your information.

Trivelin Exactly – one good thing about generous people is they anticipate your needs and spare you the humiliation of spelling them out: incredible.

Lélio I'll do what you ask, on one condition: the information must be worth paying for. Now out with it.

Trivelin Why does having money bankrupt so many people's generosity? What a curse! Although in your case I'm confident that justice will pay out what caution would prefer to claw back. Here goes then: you believe the Chevalier to be your intimate and faithful friend – am I right?

Lélio Yes – obviously.

Trivelin Big mistake.

Lélio Meaning?

Trivelin You believe that the Countess still loves you – yes?

Lélio I know she does.

Trivelin Big mistake number two.

Lélio What?

Trivelin Exactly, Monsieur: he's no friend of yours, and you're no friend of hers: the Countess has stopped loving you, the Chevalier has stolen her heart. He loves her – she loves him – been there – done it – got the T-shirt – that's my information. Now let's both turn it to our advantage.

Lélio What makes you so sure about this?

Trivelin Trust me, Monsieur: I just have to look into a woman's eyes and I can tell what she's thinking almost word for word. Every emotion's written on her face and I can read that writing as easily as I can read my own. For example, just now, while you were in the garden picking the Countess flowers, I was doing some pruning of my own in her vicinity, when I saw the Chevalier with her, laughing and acting the fool. 'Don't be so ridiculous,' she goes, with this odd little smile. Now nobody else would've even noticed that odd little smile. But for an expert like me it was a sign – and you know what it meant? – it meant, 'I really find you terribly fascinating, Chevalier, you really are an extremely attractive man. Can't you tell how much I like you?'

Lélio I see what you're saying, but how about a more concrete example for a non-expert like myself?

Trivelin Here's one that doesn't need interpreting. The Chevalier goes on like this, then snatches a few kisses, which she doesn't welcome, but fails to avoid. 'Stop it,' she goes – with this blank look on her face – but without trying to move away – as if she's too 'lazy' to defend herself – 'Stop it. You must be out of your mind.' While I just carry on with my pruning and for 'Stop it' read 'One more kiss', and for 'must be out of your mind' read 'mustn't look like I'm encouraging you but if you can't control yourself that's hardly my fault'.

Lélio I get the idea – kisses are pretty concrete.

Trivelin But here's the nicest part. 'Such a beautiful hand,' he goes. 'Please let me hold it.' 'I'd rather you didn't.' 'Oh but please.' 'I don't want you to.' But the hand is nevertheless gripped, stroked, admired. 'Stop that. No more touching.' Slaps him with a glove – which translates: 'Don't let go.' Glove is grabbed. Further assaults on first hand. Other hand tries to intervene. Further gain by the enemy. 'I don't understand. This has to stop.' 'Easier said, Madame, than done.' Countess squirms away, Chevalier meets eyes, Countess blushes. Renewed passion from man, manufactured anger from woman: man unrepentant, down on his knees. Woman half-choked by desire, man – stiff with it. Silence. I'm watching their eyes – which tell a story – but one I'd be embarrassed to repeat. 'What d'you think you're doing, Monsieur?' 'You know quite well, Madame.' 'Up off your knees.' 'You mean you forgive me?' 'Don't even ask.' That was the state of play when I left, but I imagine we can guess the final score. What d'you think?

Lélio I think your investigations are well worth following up.

Trivelin Following up? Just how far exactly am I supposed to 'follow them up'? It's one thing to observe love blossom in a garden, but to watch it bear fruit in the bedroom is another matter – assuming it hasn't already done so, given the way things were progressing.

Lélio Progressing is certainly the word.

Trivelin But isn't it incredible? If it wasn't for me you'd've married that woman! You should've seen the way she let him play with her fingers . . .

Lélio Really? You felt she was getting a taste for it.

Trivelin Yes, Monsieur. (So's he, by the look of him.) So – would you say I've earned my reward?

Lélio Definitely: you disgust me.

Trivelin 'Definitely you disgust me' – that's a strange kind of thank you.

Lélio The Chevalier would beat you unconscious if I told him you'd been spying. But listen: out of the kindness of my heart, I won't say a word. Cheer up. In lieu of cash, I'll spare you a beating. (*He goes.*)

SCENE FOUR

Trivelin.

Trivelin I've heard of the cashless economy, but this is ridiculous. Thank you so much, Monsieur. And may you continue to get rich at my expense. Of all the tricks life's played on me, this is certainly the most grotesque. 'Spare me a beating in lieu of cash' – takes tight-fistedness to new extremes. I just don't understand: I tell him his best friend's all over the woman he loves – he asks me if she's getting a taste for it. Is Little Miss Chevalier taking me for a ride? Are the two of them more intimate than I thought?

SCENE FIVE

Arlequin, Trivelin.

Trivelin (Let's see if Arlequin knows anything.) Hey! Arlequin! Where're you going?

Arlequin To see if my master's had any letters.

Trivelin You look lost – what's on your mind?

Arlequin Money.

Trivelin Always a rich topic of debate.

Arlequin And also I was looking for you.

Trivelin Oh? What d'you want?

Arlequin To discuss money.

Trivelin Money money money – clearly an obsession.

Arlequin Tell me, my friend, where did you find all that cash I saw you pull out of your pocket to pay for the bottle of wine we drank earlier on in the village? You must have a secret recipe for making it.

Trivelin For making it, no – for spending it, yes.

Arlequin I've got a recipe for that – you just have to go out drinking.

Trivelin Absolutely – drinking's an important element – but the process is greatly speeded up by stirring in some attractive women.

Arlequin Attractive women? You won't find that ingredient in this kitchen.

Trivelin There'll be other kitchens, my friend. But listen: I've got a question of my own: are your master and the Chevalier best of friends?

Arlequin Yes.

Trivelin Really? Would you say they were especially close? What kind of things do they say to each other?

Arlequin Say? Things like: 'How are you today?' 'Very well, thank you. And yourself?' 'Fine, thanks.' Then they have lunch, then they have dinner, then they say

'Goodnight.' 'Goodnight. Sleep well.' Then they go to bed, then they go to sleep, then they wake up and start all over again. What're they supposed to say?

Trivelin Nothing, my friend. I just needed to check with you, because of recent developments.

Arlequin Oh?

Trivelin Yes – there's a young lady here I'm emotionally attached to – and the deeper our masters' friendship, the longer will be the attachment. Understood?

Arlequin And where does this lady with the long attachment live?

Trivelin Here. I've just told you. It's serious.

Arlequin Oh joy! Pretty?

Trivelin Pretty? What an incompetent adjective! You're not doing her justice. She is beautiful, adorable, and no less than I deserve.

Arlequin (*moved*) Oh my darling! Oh my foil-wrapped little chocolate!

Trivelin And hers is the sweet hand that gave me the money – made even more precious for being her gift.

Arlequin (*hearing this, drops his arms*) I can't bear it.

Trivelin (He makes me laugh – let's see if I can't reduce him to total jelly.) And that's not all, my friend. She talks to me like an angel. She finds me so desirable, she makes me blush. 'Tell me you love me,' she says. 'Tell me you want me.'

Arlequin (*rapt*) I want you, I want you.

Trivelin And while she's saying all this, desperate to prove she means it, she's rummaging in her pocket to pull out those exquisite francs. 'Take them' she says, trying to force them into my hand. And when I won't, she gets angry: 'Go on!' she shouts. 'Take them. These are just a foretaste of the treasures in store.' At which point I swallow my pride – and force myself to accept.

Arlequin (*throws down his bat and belt, and falls to his knees*) Please – friend – I'm down on my knees in all humility begging for just one glimpse of this incomparably moneyed child whose love includes a free cash gift. Maybe she'd give me a foretaste too. Please: just one glimpse – one glance – one tiny tiny glimpse before I die.

Trivelin Can't be done, friend. What's possible for me remains unthinkable for you. There's a world of difference between the true pedigree and a mongrel like yourself.

Arlequin Just show me the girl . . .

Trivelin Can't be done. But because I like you, you can share in my good fortune. Starting from now I'll sponsor you to the tune of one bottle of red per day.

Arlequin (*half in tears*) A bottle a day – that's thirty bottles a month. In my hour of need, give me my first month's sponsorship in advance.

Trivelin I'm afraid each bottle must be drunk under my personal supervision.

Arlequin (*moves off, crying*) So I'll never see my darling. Where are you hiding, my sweet moneyed angel? I'm coming to find you . . . (*Cries, then matter of fact.*) Just the first day's then.

Trivelin I can't – here's my master. You go and wait for me.

Arlequin goes, and starts crying again.

Chevalier, Trivelin.

Trivelin (*a moment alone, laughing*) The poor boy's totally out of his depth. He's best kept out of this.

   Chevalier appears.

Trivelin So there you are, man like no other. How is our plan progressing?

Chevalier (*as if angry*) Extremely well, 'Monsieur' Trivelin. But I have to say I am very disappointed in you.

Trivelin You may be disappointed, but you don't have to say it.

Chevalier In a word, you disgust me.

Trivelin Don't worry: it's a typical reaction.

Chevalier You're a hypocrite who I will severely punish.

Trivelin It's part of the learning curve, that's all.

Chevalier What exactly were you playing at, telling Lélio I love the Countess?

Trivelin What? You mean he told you what I said?

Chevalier Well naturally.

Trivelin Well then I'm rather pleased. To pay for the information he promised to keep his mouth shut – now he's opened it, he's in my debt.

Chevalier Typical. You mean this was to get money out of him, you scum.

Trivelin Scum? Such exquisite French! Such dazzling use of the language! I wanted money – that's all.

Chevalier But hadn't I given you money?

Trivelin And hadn't I gratefully accepted it? Just what is your problem? Is your money really so antisocial? Can't it make friends with Lélio's?

Chevalier You take care: one more piece of insolence like that and you'll have my mistress to deal with.

Trivelin Don't – I was indiscreet – I apologise – I've been weak – please: seal my lips with a kiss.

Chevalier Out of the question.

Trivelin With something else, then.

Chevalier No.

Trivelin You don't seem to understand – you're not really asking me to spell it out?

Chevalier takes out his watch.

Aha! – good clue – not a watch – but close: made of metal and lives in your pocket.

Chevalier All right, all right, I understand.

Trivelin Although I'd rather have a kiss.

Chevalier Take this – and in future behave yourself.

Trivelin You're a very bad girl. You promise so much, and deliver so little – but so exquisitely, I can't resist.

SCENE SEVEN

Chevalier, Trivelin, Arlequin.

Arlequin has appeared and overheard the end of the previous scene. As Chevalier passes money to Trivelin,

Arlequin with one hand intercepts it, and with the other takes the Chevalier and kisses him.

Arlequin Yes! Yes! Got her! My sweet golden nugget! Trivelin! I'm so happy, I'm losing my mind!

Trivelin And I'm losing my money.

Arlequin Let me look at you, my adorable cash box. So pretty! Come on, gorgeous – my poor heart – I'm having a crisis. Quickly. Cure me. A foretaste is all it takes. (*He laughs.*)

Chevalier (*to Trivelin*) Just get rid of him. What does he mean, 'foretaste'?

Trivelin Typical, typical – he's asking for money.

Chevalier Well, if that's all he wants, take him away, and tell him to keep his mouth shut. (*to Arlequin*) My dear Arlequin, don't give me away. I promise you as many foretastes as you can manage. Trivelin will see to it. But talk and you get nothing.

Arlequin I'll be good, little man. Will you love me?

Chevalier I'll try to.

Trivelin Come on, friend: I'm your sponsor, remember? How about that drink?

Arlequin (*doesn't move*) Yes, how about it?

Trivelin Well, come on, then. (*to Chevalier*) Do what you have to – everything's under control.

Arlequin (*as he goes*) What a peach! What a peach!

Countess, Chevalier.

Chevalier (*alone for a moment*) Whatever happens, I'm enjoying this too much to just suddenly stop. I don't mind about the money: what's interesting is to see how far I can take this. Here comes the Countess – let's find out what she really feels about me. You don't look happy, Madame – what's wrong?

Countess (Let's see what he really thinks.) I'm afraid I have to make a suggestion which displeases me, but to which I have no alternative.

Chevalier An unfortunate start to our conversation, Madame.

Countess You've probably noticed I've enjoyed your company here – and – if it were purely up to me – I could imagine enjoying it a good deal more.

Chevalier I understand. No need to explain: I'll go straight back to Paris.

Countess Please don't be cross with me: I have my reasons.

Chevalier Which I shan't question: you give an order, I obey it.

Countess You're not to call it an order.

Chevalier Please – Madame – I don't deserve this degree of tact – you're far too kind.

Countess I repeat: it's not an order. And if you would rather stay, then obviously a man in your position has every right to.

Chevalier Yes obviously – but I don't want to take advantage of the fact I make you feel uncomfortable.

Countess I don't see, Chevalier, how you can take advantage of something you're probably imagining.

Chevalier Do you really have to be so ambiguous?

Countess Do you really have to be so obtuse as to find me ambiguous? I'm a woman. I'm forced to be. I can ask you to stay, but I can't be any more explicit: the rest's up to you.

Chevalier (Her self-respect's fading – let's demolish it.) In which case: goodbye. I'm tempted to stay – for obvious reasons – but I'd rather leave than be victim of a dangerous misunderstanding. You're looking at a man who is emotionally confused.

Countess More like a man who is emotionally illiterate.

Chevalier (*turning back*) Please, Madame, at least wait till I've gone before expressing your contempt.

Countess I'm afraid, Monsieur, I couldn't help myself. Go back to your precious Paris and women who make their intentions only too clear, who beg men to stay with them in no uncertain terms, who blush at nothing. Not me – I can't – I've too much pride. And if you leave, it will be because of this mania of yours for taking everything the wrong way.

Chevalier Would you be happy if I stayed?

Countess You can't ask a woman for a yes or no answer! Such stark alternatives! Could anything be more detestable than a man who can't work it out for himself? Leave me alone – I'm tired of always taking the lead.

Chevalier (*pretending to go*) I've worked it out – I'm going.

Countess He's worked it out, he says, he's worked it out and off he goes: incredible insight! I can't think how I ever found him attractive. Lélio can leave too – I've had enough: I'm sick of it – sick of their total incompetence. I detest men. They're unbearable. I'll manage without.

Chevalier (*as if he's thought of something*) I completely forgot to ask, Madame, if there's anything I can do for you in Paris.

Countess There most certainly is: forget I ever asked you to stay.

Chevalier But if you want me to forget, then you can't really want me to leave. Am I right?

Countess What? You actually understand? It's a miracle. (If I wasn't prepared to be so frank I can see we'd never get anywhere.)

Chevalier I love you, but expect nothing in return.

Countess You're quite right to expect nothing in return.

Chevalier In which case, Madame, it's pointless my staying.

Countess Pointless? The way he twists things. I have to watch every little word.

Chevalier Perhaps – but why can't you just say what you mean? I leave – you make me stay – I assume it's going to be worth my while – on the contrary, it's so you can tell me to 'expect nothing'. What kind of encouragement is that? I'm sorry, Madame, but I don't intend to live like this – I can't – I love you too much.

Countess This love of yours seems rather violent – I hope it knows when to stop.

Chevalier How can love stop when you've started it?

44

Countess Listen: what is it you want?

Chevalier For you to feel something.

Countess In that case, you'll have to be patient.

Chevalier Me? Patient? No – I'm sorry – patience is a featureless desert – and I don't have a map.

Countess Be brave, be brave, you won't get lost.

Chevalier Make your heart my companion, and I'd go anywhere.

Countess Hmm – we might not get very far together.

Chevalier Why? What makes you say that?

Countess Because I suspect you're fickle.

Chevalier You had me frightened: I thought you had a more serious objection. As for being fickle, if that's all that's holding you back, let's leave now: when you know me more intimately, that's not the first word that will spring to mind.

Countess Let's discuss this rationally: I do feel very attracted, I won't deny that: but is this kind of sudden attraction normal?

Chevalier No. But nothing's normal when it comes to love. I want your heart to be mine, and I'm prepared to earn it in whatever way I can – normal or not.

Countess Trust me – I'm generous – maybe I'll make a gift of it.

Chevalier Cross out 'maybe' – the sense will be sweeter.

Countess Let's leave it in – maybe it's meaningless.

Chevalier Put that way, it sounds more acceptable.

Countess Well 'maybe' I wanted it to.

Chevalier The point is: are you likely to love me?

Countess I could equally ask, do *you* love *me*?

Chevalier I do, Madame – at immense personal cost.

Countess But you've known me such a short time – I still can't help feeling surprised.

Chevalier Surprised? Day breaks – the sun rises – does that surprise you too? Because I just don't know what I'm supposed to say – well? How could a man who's seen you for even one moment fail to adore you?

Countess I believe you – stop being so angry – stop attacking me.

Chevalier Yes, Countess, I love you, and of all men capable of love, I swear by this beautiful hand, as it surrenders to my caress, there's not one whose love is purer, or more refined. Look, Madame, let your beautiful eyes look into mine: don't cheat me of their delicious confusion. Ah! So deep! So utterly inviting! Who'd've believed those eyes would one day be staring into mine.

Countess Stop this – give me back my hand – you can say what you have to say perfectly well without it.

Chevalier You let me take it: let me keep it.

Countess All right – I'll wait till you've finished.

Chevalier I'll never be finished.

Countess You're making me forget what I was going to say – I came especially, and you keep distracting me. Let's be clear: you love me, which is very good, but what are we going to do? Lélio's jealous.

Chevalier Well, so am I – that's two of us.

Countess He suspects you're in love with me.

Chevalier Only a fool would 'suspect' – he should be convinced.

Countess And he's worried I might love you.

Chevalier Well why shouldn't you? The man's an idiot. Just tell him he's right, and his worries will be over.

Countess I have to believe it before I can say it.

Chevalier What? – What about the gift you just promised?

Countess I said maybe.

Chevalier I knew that nasty little word was going to cause trouble. So? What exactly is the alternative? – if you don't love me? Marry Lélio?

Countess Lélio is starting to irritate.

Chevalier Tell him to stop, then, and leave us alone.

Countess He's the most odd kind of person.

Chevalier The most tedious kind of man.

Countess And so rough and on edge – I really don't know how to take him.

Chevalier My advice is cautiously.

Countess He doesn't appeal to the mind, and he's stopped appealing to the heart.

Chevalier Then break it off.

Countess Is that your advice? Because I think I'm going to be forced to.

Chevalier Exactly – but where does that leave your heart?

Countess None of your business.

Chevalier Of course it's my business.

Countess You'll be informed.

Chevalier Jesus Christ!

Countess What's wrong?

Chevalier Just your incredible way of drawing things out.

Countess Then stop being so impatient, Chevalier. I never met a man like it.

Chevalier Well I'm afraid that's simply the kind of man I am.

Countess Wait. I need to know you better.

Chevalier I love you and worship you – what else is there to know? But look, if it will make you happier: if you feel nothing, tell me to leave – I'll leave and we'll never mention this again. But if there's hope for me, don't even speak, don't say a word: silence will be my reward – and it won't cost you a single syllable.

Countess Ah!

Chevalier Now I'm happy.

Countess But I came to tell you to leave – Lélio said –

Chevalier Forget Lélio – he's a lost cause.

SCENE NINE

Chevalier, Countess, Lélio.

Lélio appears, making positive signs to Chevalier.

Lélio Charming, Monsieur le Chevalier, utterly charming – 'lost cause', am I? Your contempt for me is all too clear, but cuts no ice, I can assure you, with this good lady.

Lélio – who is the better man – stays right here – and it is you, Monsieur, who leaves. It's incredible! What d'you make of him, Madame? Is this what he calls playing by the rules? Is this acceptable behaviour?

Chevalier And what exactly, Monsieur, is wrong with my behaviour? When I became your friend, did I take a vow of chastity? Did I promise to blind myself to all the grace and beauty of this world? No, I did not! Your friendship's all well and good, but – compared to my love for this lady – entirely dispensable. You find you have a rival? Then learn to live with it. Are you really surprised to discover that a woman might have a mind of her own? I can see you don't like surprises – but I suggest you start getting used to them.

Lélio I've nothing to say to you. Madame's disdain will be punishment enough. (*to Countess*) Would you care to take my hand, since I'm sure you find this gentleman's conversation less than amusing.

Countess (*serious, moving away*) What is it you want from me? I've no complaint with the Chevalier. If he loves me, he puts it impeccably. The worst I could accuse him of is the mediocrity of his taste.

Chevalier More people would share my taste than would support your accusation, Madame.

Lélio (*angry*) Oh delightful. Just what role exactly am I supposed to be playing here? I thought the plan was to get married, but now, Madame . . .

Countess Please. I dislike anger. We'll talk when you've calmed down.

She leaves.

SCENE TEN

Chevalier, Lélio.

Lélio watches the Countess leave. When she's out of sight, he bursts out laughing.

Lélio Stupid, stupid woman. What d'you think? Not bad jealous acting, eh?

The Countess deliberately comes back to see what's happening.

(*under his breath*) She's watching us. (*out loud*) Just wait and see, Chevalier, you just wait and see.

Chevalier (*under his breath*) Incredible hypocrite. (*out loud*) Goodbye, Lélio. We'll settle this whichever way you like – and that's a promise.

They leave in separate directions.

Act Three

Lélio, Arlequin.

Arlequin Terrible terrible terrible.

Lélio What's terrible? What're you talking about?

Arlequin Terrible terrible terrible terrible.

Lélio What exactly has happened?

Arlequin Ah, Monsieur – it's so terrible I'll never laugh again.

Lélio Why not?

Arlequin Because I'm so sad.

Lélio Sad about what?

Arlequin About it being so terrible.

Lélio But what's made everything so sad and terrible? Has somebody hurt you?

Arlequin Yes, very much.

Lélio What, did they beat you?

Arlequin Beat me? Much worse than that.

Lélio Much worse than that?

Arlequin Yes. When a poor man loses money, he loses his will to live – and so have I – I'm going to die.

Lélio What d'you mean, money?

Arlequin Ready cash – that's what I mean.

Lélio And you had some?

Arlequin Yes, yes – honestly. When I had it I was so happy. And now it's gone it's so terrible.

Lélio And who exactly had given you this ready cash?

Arlequin It was Monsieur le Chevalier gave me a foretaste.

Lélio What foretaste?

Arlequin I've just said!

Lélio God give me strength! Arlequin, if somebody's hurt you, I'll deal with it – but first let's be clear. You said money – then you called it a foretaste: I don't understand, so I want a precise answer. Has the Chevalier been giving you money?

Arlequin No not to me but he gave it to Trivelin to give it to me but Trivelin didn't give it to me he gave it all to himself and he didn't give me anything.

Lélio Is this a lot of money? How much exactly was it?

Arlequin Maybe four or five hundred francs – I wasn't counting.

Lélio Four or five hundred? Why did the Chevalier give you so much money?

Arlequin Because I asked for a foretaste.

Lélio Please: not the foretaste.

Arlequin Yes yes – honestly. Because the Chevalier had given one to Trivelin.

Lélio (I've no idea what he's talking about, but something's not right.) Listen: did you do something for the Chevalier in return for payment?

Arlequin No, but I was jealous of the way he loved Trivelin, and stuffed his purse with money, and had such

52

a special relationship – and I wanted to be stuffed with a special relationship too.

Lélio Just what kind of gobbledegook is this?

Arlequin It's all God's honest truth.

Lélio What d'you mean, a special relationship? What're you trying to say about Trivelin and the Chevalier? You make it sound like the Chevalier's a woman.

Arlequin Only because he could make mincemeat out of your heart if you found out who he was. Go on – try it – say, 'I know who you are and I'll keep it a secret.' If you don't get a foretaste straight away, then I'm a Dutchman.

Lélio I don't understand. Who're you saying the Chevalier is?

Arlequin I'm not – that's the whole point of the secret.

Lélio Which is what I'm asking you to tell me.

Arlequin I'd be ruined, Monsieur – he'd give me no more money – and if people found out about his feminine side, he'd be very very angry.

Lélio What feminine side? What makes the Chevalier so special?

Arlequin Ah, Monsieur! There's no man quite like him – not in the whole wide world – but he hides it by play-acting.

Lélio Play-acting? Everything he says confirms my worst suspicions: the way the Chevalier looks, the strange way he smiles . . . But here comes Trivelin. If he knows the truth I'll force it out of him. He'll be more coherent than this idiot. (*to Arlequin*) You can go. I'll see what I can do about your money.

Arlequin goes, kissing his hand, whimpering.

53

SCENE TWO

Lélio, Trivelin.

Trivelin (*enters lost in thought, sees Lélio and says*)
There's Mr Cashless Economy. Just the sight of him sets
my teeth on edge. (*Moves away.*) The man's best avoided.

Lélio (*calls him*) Trivelin – I'd like a word with you.

Trivelin Me, Monsieur? Couldn't it wait? I've got this
terrible headache that makes conversation difficult.

Lélio Nobody's interested in your headaches. I said,
come here.

Trivelin The thing is – honestly – I've nothing new to
report – I mean it.

Lélio (*goes and takes him by the arm*) We need to talk.

Trivelin What about? Feeling guilty about the way you
paid me? Or should I say failed to? I know it's a minor
detail – but that's where the devil is – I mean in the
detail – am I right?

Lélio Listen: cut the bullshit.

Trivelin I warned you you'd got me on a bad day.

Lélio I just want you to answer some simple questions.
Tell me the truth, and I'll make it worth your while.

Trivelin Or in other words not beat me senseless.

Lélio I will be brief, and I expect you to be succinct.
Understood?

Trivelin Understood. No comment. Succinct enough?

Lélio Don't you dare talk to me like that.

Trivelin (*moving away*) Fine.

Lélio Where're you going?

Trivelin If you don't want me to talk, the simplest thing's for me to leave.

Lélio I'm getting bored with this, bored and angry. Stay right where you are, and answer my questions.

Trivelin (What the fuck is this man's problem?)

Lélio What's that you're muttering?

Trivelin Involuntary reflex, Monsieur.

Lélio Look here, Trivelin, let's try and discuss this calmly, shall we?

Trivelin Absolutely – like the gentlemen we are.

Lélio Have you known the Chevalier long?

Trivelin Not long at all – for as long as I've known you.

Lélio D'you know who he is?

Trivelin He says he's the youngest son of an aristocratic family, and that his elder brother inherited the money – but I've never seen the birth certificate. If I do I'll make you a copy.

Lélio I want you to be completely open.

Trivelin I am being open: I'll make you a copy – you have my absolutely non-negotiable word on it.

Lélio You're not telling the truth: the Chevalier is not what he claims.

Trivelin You mean he's the eldest? And there's me believing he's the impoverished youngest. Typical.

Lélio Don't try and be clever. Admit you love this so-called Chevalier.

Trivelin Well, of course I love him – it's my duty to love my fellow man.

Lélio Doing your duty seems to give you an inordinate pleasure.

Trivelin That, Monsieur, is where you're completely wrong. Nothing could be more onerous. I'm rigorous about trivia, but show me a moral obligation and I run a mile. Isn't that society all over? I'm sure you're the same.

Lélio (*angry*) Don't you lie to me. You're in love with the Chevalier.

Trivelin Whoa there! This is serious.

Lélio You know his true sex.

Trivelin True sex? Is that like true love? I'm not sure I'm familiar with / that expression.

Lélio (*aggressively*) Just you listen to me. If you play any more of these games, I'll have you beaten to death. Do I make myself clear?

Trivelin Very.

Lélio Do not antagonise me. I have a great deal at stake here: money and property. Either you talk, or you die.

Trivelin Die if I don't talk? Well then, a man with a mouth like mine is obviously going to live for ever.

Lélio Talk then.

Trivelin Tell you what – you pick a subject – any subject – and I'd be happy to discuss it.

Lélio Are you refusing? You need to be taught a lesson.

Trivelin (*as if afraid*) Christ! If you didn't have such a respectable-looking face I'd be terrified.

Lélio (*looks at him*) You piece of shit.

Trivelin It's my clothes, Monsieur, that are shit. I'm a decent enough human being, but integrity's wasted in an outfit like this. Its value is morally and financially zero.

Lélio All right – I'm not going to force you. But I know where to find you – and if things turn out badly, I'll hold you responsible.

Trivelin Wherever we may happen to meet, Monsieur, I will always be delighted to doff my hat, as proof of my profound, and, may I say, ever-deepening respect.

Lélio (*angry*) You can go.

Trivelin (*going*) Which is precisely what I wanted to do in the first place.

SCENE THREE

Chevalier, Lélio (lost in thought).

Chevalier Well well, my friend: the Countess is writing letters. Then she says she'd like to take a walk with me. So I just wanted to warn you not to interrupt, but lurk somewhere and look appropriately jealous. What I'm hoping is that I can bring things to a head, and force her to commit. But I did have one small concern: is the contract she gave you completely watertight? Because some contracts aren't worth the paper they're written on. I understand law, so if I could see it, and there's a problem, we could take steps.

Lélio (Let's see if my suspicions are justified.)

Chevalier Well? Is something wrong?

Lélio I don't have the contract with me. But there's something else we should talk about.

Chevalier Oh? You mean some other woman you'd like to marry me off to?

Lélio Something rather more serious: fighting a duel.

Chevalier God – when you say serious you really mean it. So who exactly has been challenging your moral authority?

Lélio This is not a joke.

Chevalier (Has Arlequin talked?) Well if you go through with it, please mention me in the will.

Lélio Blood will be spilt – and it won't be my own.

Chevalier I see blood on a regular basis. It's not something I personally have a problem with.

Lélio Well I have a personal problem with you, Monsieur – and yours is the blood I intend to spill.

Chevalier Mine?

Lélio Precisely.

Chevalier (*laughs and pushes him away*) You need to lie down – you're a sick man.

Lélio Come with me.

Chevalier (*feels Lélio's pulse*) Your pulse is all over the place – must be sunstroke.

Lélio Don't make excuses. What I said was: come with me.

Chevalier You're having an attack, my friend – you need to rest.

Lélio If you won't come, you're beneath contempt.

Chevalier (*with sympathy*) Poor man – you're clearly not in control of what you're saying – at least I hope not.

Lélio You're acting like some pathetic girl.

Chevalier (Let's be brave.) Lélio, I accept you're sick. But if you're not, then be very, very careful.

Lélio (*with disdain*) You're a ridiculous coward. You don't need a sword, you need a sewing kit.

Chevalier Pass me some scissors and I'll cut your heart out.

Lélio Oh really? Without fainting?

Chevalier Without even blinking. But listen – I'm getting carried away – maybe you're still feverish. Let's see your eyes. (*Lélio looks at him*) Hmm. Definitely a mad look – but obviously I was wrong. At least let me know why you're so keen to be taught a lesson.

Lélio See those trees? I'll tell you when we get there.

Chevalier In which case let's go. (If he sees I'm serious, he may back down.)

They both walk away. Then, when they're close to going out:

Lélio (*turns round, looks at Chevalier*) So you're coming, are you?

Chevalier What d'you mean, coming? Of course I'm coming. Don't try and back out of it. Because you've had your chance, Lélio, and whether you're sick, or whether you're not, is now immaterial. I'll cut you into so many pieces with my so-called sewing kit, even the doctors will be confused. Let's go.

Lélio (*scrutinising him*) You really mean that?

Chevalier Let's stop wasting time – you've an appointment to keep.

Lélio (*coming back*) Calm down, my friend, we need to discuss this.

Chevalier (*grabbing his hand*) Because you're the one who's beneath contempt.

Lélio (Christ, I was wrong. He's not just a man, he's a dangerous one.)

Chevalier (*persists*) You're the pathetic girl.

Lélio No – stop – listen: the fact is I really thought you *were* one. Don't you realise how pretty you look? There are women who'd sell their souls for a face like that. It's incredibly deceptive.

Chevalier It's not me who's deceptive – come on (*i.e. fight*).

Lélio No – I just needed to test you: you got Trivelin to give money to Arlequin – I don't understand why.

Chevalier (*serious*) Because he overheard me talking about our plan, and might've told the Countess – that's why, Monsieur.

Lélio I had no idea. And Arlequin talked about you as if you were a girl, something your looks had already made me think about. But I was wrong: you're not just good-looking, you're brave as well. Let's put this behind us, shall we?

Chevalier Once a man like myself's been provoked, he likes to cause maximum damage.

Lélio Which is another female characteristic you have.

Chevalier Still, I've no desire to kill anyone. Let's say the insult never happened – provided you apologise.

Lélio Unreservedly, Chevalier – and please forget the rash things I said.

Chevalier Of course – and I'm delighted to be spared the embarrassment of killing a fellow human being. It may be illegal for men to fight duels, but believe me, as far as I'm concerned, illegality is no deterrent.

Lélio I can well believe it.

Chevalier You trust me, then?

Lélio Like a brother. (*Offers his hand.*) Let's shake on it.

SCENE FOUR

Chevalier, Lélio, Arlequin.

Arlequin Pardon me interrupting, Monsieur Chevalier, but that thief Trivelin won't let me have the money you gave him to pass on to me. And I've been so so discreet. You gave strict instructions not to say you're a girl and Monsieur Lélio here knows how careful I've been, because I haven't breathed – have I, Monsieur – haven't breathed a single word – and never will.

Chevalier (*appalled*) Stupid idiot – don't you see what you've just done?

Arlequin (*unhappily*) Don't say idiot. That's not how to love somebody. (*to Lélio*) Please, Monsieur, I can explain. I turn up here and Trivelin's saying to him, 'Sweetheart, you're so pretty, kiss me.' 'No.' 'Then give me the money.' So he puts out his hand to take it, so I put out my hand and the money falls into it. So the Chevalier sees me and he goes, 'My child,' he goes, 'don't let on that I'm basically a girl.' So I go, 'Of course not, darling, just promise me love.' 'I promise,' she goes. Then she tells Trivelin to give me a foretaste and we go for a drink and we have a few drinks and I come all the way back

61

to collect my money and cash in my love and she turns round and calls me an idiot!

The Chevalier is thinking.

Lélio That will do. Leave us. And keep your mouth shut.

Arlequin (*goes*) Mind you take care of my investment.

SCENE FIVE

Chevalier, Lélio.

Lélio Well, Mr Duellist, it seems your female characteristics are more extensive than previously thought. Or am I wrong?

Chevalier No. Everything he said was true.

Lélio Which puts you in a rather difficult position, sweetheart.

Chevalier I beg your pardon? It does no such thing. I'm a woman, and will defend my reputation.

Lélio Absolutely – but what exactly is your business here?

Chevalier Admit it was bad luck. Admit I had you completely fooled. Afraid of a 'pathetic girl' – I find that hilarious.

Lélio That's not the issue. I made the mistake of opening my heart to you.

Chevalier Don't worry – I find its contents remarkably unattractive.

Lélio You know my plans.

Chevalier Plans you didn't intend to share with this particular confidante – am I right?

Lélio Indeed.

Chevalier But they're wonderful! I especially like the way the wife turns ugly and gets packed off to the country two weeks after the wedding. Quite brilliant.

Lélio You've an excellent memory – but let's move on. Who are you?

Chevalier A young woman, and, as you yourself said, quite a pretty one, who intends to remain attractive for some while yet, provided my future husband spares me the country-house treatment. That's who I am. What's more, I'm almost as sick and twisted as you are.

Lélio More so, in my humble opinion.

Chevalier No – please – you're far too modest.

Lélio Why exactly are you here?

Chevalier To paint your portrait so that a certain lady can decide how to deal with the sitter.

Lélio How artistic.

Chevalier Very. And this portrait means an innocent lamb escapes the wolf, and twelve hundred thousand francs a year are spared an unholy alliance. Not a bad outcome for a simple disguise.

Lélio (*intrigued*) What exactly are you trying to say?

Chevalier I'll explain. The lamb is my mistress, the twelve hundred thousand francs the income on her property – the 'arithmetic' we spoke about – and the wolf, Monsieur, who would've devoured it all, is yourself.

Lélio Jesus! I'm ruined!

Chevalier Not ruined – cheated of your prey, that's all. Of course it was certainly quite juicy – but don't blame me – you're the wolf. My mistress knows you've gone to Paris incognito, and becomes suspicious. She has you followed and finds out about the ball. Knowing I'm sly and intelligent, she gets me invited. She dresses me like this so I can probe your character. I arrive, do as I'm told, become your friend, probe your character, discover it's worthless. That's my report: no redeeming features.

Lélio You mean you're this lady's personal attendant?

Chevalier And your very humble servant.

Lélio If I'm honest, I feel bad about this.

Chevalier Honest? D'you mean bad about what you tried to do, or bad about the fact you didn't succeed?

Lélio Let's change the subject, shall we? Why go on seducing the Countess? Why agree to take on that particular role with her?

Chevalier For one excellent reason. You were trying to get ten million out of her – am I right? For which you needed my complicity. So when I was close to achieving a result, my plan was to apply some gentle pressure and share in the winnings. Either by innocently asking to see the contract, walking off with it, then selling it back to you for cash – or alternatively by threatening to expose your 'calculations', effectively reducing them to zero. Oh, it was all immaculately planned: cash in hand, I'd be off like a shot, then sell my little character sketch to a grateful mistress. Add to that the small bits of money I've managed to save out of wages et cetera, and what with my good looks I was turning into a pretty desirable commodity – before Mr Wolf came along. Now it's all spoiled, and I'm really quite angry – although I do have some sympathy for your position.

Lélio Look – if you still wanted to . . .

Chevalier Wanted to what? Go on.

Lélio You could end up with even more than you originally thought.

Chevalier Well, listen: I won't be a hypocrite. I'm not above behaving badly, any more than you are. Make me rich and I'll say you're the perfect gentleman – but only on the understanding that a lie of that magnitude doesn't come cheap.

Lélio Whatever you like – name your price.

Chevalier Strictly between ourselves, then. I want two million francs, not a penny less. In return I finish with the Countess, and leave my mistress entirely in your hands. If this is acceptable, I will send tonight, to Paris, a letter which you yourself can dictate. Describe yourself in whatever glowing terms you like – I shan't interfere. When you're married, act as you wish – I'll be rich and so will you. The others can learn to live with it.

Lélio The two million's yours – as is my everlasting friendship.

Chevalier I'd rather have an extra five thousand francs.

Lélio My dear girl, I'll give you ten.

Chevalier Even better – more, one might say, than your friendship's actually worth.

Lélio So we write the letter tonight?

Chevalier Yes – but when do I get the money?

Lélio (*pulls off ring*) Well, to start with, this takes care of the ten thousand francs.

Chevalier Very good. But what about the two million?

Lélio I'll sign you an agreement presently.

Chevalier Presently? The Countess will be here any moment and I refuse to go on without watertight guarantees. Let me have the contract you signed with her – then 'presently' we can swap it for your agreement.

Lélio (*takes it out*) All right. Take it.

Chevalier You'd better not give me away.

Lélio Don't be mad.

Chevalier Here's the Countess. When I've talked to her, come back angrily and insist that she decides between us once and for all.

Lélio goes.

SCENE SIX

Countess, Chevalier.

Chevalier I wanted to speak to you, Countess.

Countess You made me nervous, Chevalier. I saw Lélio talking to you. The man's out of control – please – keep away from him.

Chevalier He's certainly a character. D'you know he's boasting he can make you get rid of me.

Countess Get rid of himself would be more intelligent.

Chevalier I told him that – but I need your support. Let's do it. Get rid of him.

Countess You're too reckless, Chevalier, you've stopped being reasonable.

Chevalier Reasonable? What's being reasonable got to do with it? Love goes on regardless. If you've still got room for reason – and how could you be so hurtful? – then you'll never have room for love.

Countess Another one of your strange little outbursts – terribly attractive – but of course you know that. You fascinate me. You and Lélio are so very very different!

Chevalier More than you might imagine. But about Lélio: what I said to you was send him away immediately. Love demands it – and when love speaks, you obey.

Countess Oh really? And what if I rebel?

Chevalier You'd never dare.

Countess Never dare? The shameless way he says it!

Chevalier No – never – because the fact is you love me, and your heart is mine. I'll do whatever I want with it, just as you can do whatever you please with mine: those are the rules – which you will observe – because I say so.

Countess He's certainly not short of self-confidence. 'You love me.' 'Your heart is mine.' It all comes out so fluently it's hard not to believe he's right.

Chevalier There is absolutely no doubt in my mind, and my confidence is the confidence you've given me – simple faith in the fact that Lélio must go.

Countess You're still not thinking. I can't tell a man to simply leave!

Chevalier You can't deny me what's rightfully mine!

Countess Bully!

Chevalier Coward!

Countess Tyrant!

Chevalier Rebel – do you surrender?

Countess My dear Chevalier, I can't. I have certain reasons for treating him more delicately.

Chevalier Reasons, Madame? What reasons? What exactly are you trying to say?

Countess Calm down. The thing is is that I've lent him money.

Chevalier So? You mean there's no proper acknowledgement of the debt?

Countess On the contrary: I have it from him in writing.

Chevalier Then go to a lawyer – get it back.

Countess You're right, only the thing is . . .

Chevalier The thing? What thing? You sound embarrassed.

Countess Well, how d'you expect me to sound? To guarantee the loan, I agreed the two of us would sign a contract before marriage for the same amount.

Chevalier A contract, Madame! Oh how passionate! A true testament of love! Profound – poetic – I'm completely overwhelmed.

Countess That horrible contract, why on earth did I sign it? To be so taken in by a man I always knew I'd come to detest. I'd always felt a certain antipathy towards him, but never found the courage to act on it.

Chevalier Well, clearly he found a way to convert your so-called antipathy into its exact opposite. I can just see him now, Madame, kneeling at your feet while you joyfully listen, swearing his eternal adoration while you swear yours, searching for your mouth and your mouth opening to his – isn't that so? I see your body quiver, I see your eyes meet his, see them burn, see them melt, see

68

them brim, brim over with desire. While I stare at death – since those scenes are the death of me. How can I get this contract out of my mind? When will it stop haunting me? The pain it's going to cost! And the insane things it's making me say!

Countess Don't call it insanity, Monsieur, unless it's madness simply to be in love. I wish I'd never told you about that wretched contract. What made me think you'd behave rationally? Why did we have to meet? What have I done to be spoken to like this? How can you possibly complain? How can you say I don't love you enough? Why must you go on and on and on about Lélio? Isn't it obvious that no man's dearer to me than you are, no man more worthy, no man more certain of my enduring love? But oh no – nothing's ever enough – you get angry, refuse to listen – hurt me – punish me. What are you trying to do to us? Is this any way to live? Is it? Well, is it?

Chevalier (My shamelessness has been surprisingly successful.) I've stopped, Countess – your agony has restored my peace of mind. What loving words you've spoken – words, believe me, I would once have thought inconceivable. Let's both calm down, shall we, and forget that we argued.

Countess Why do I love you so intensely? What is it about you?

Chevalier Perhaps you should ask: what is it about yourself?

Countess But there must be something that makes you so exceptionally attractive.

Chevalier As a man, it's true, I am somewhat unique – and it's exactly those unique characteristics that mean I'll find your love hard to satisfy.

Countess You mean you don't feel worthy?

Chevalier It's too complicated to explain.

Countess Don't stop loving me, that's all I ask.

Chevalier Can your taste really be so plain?

Countess Don't hurt me any more, and I'll be happy.

Chevalier I promise; but get rid of Lélio.

Countess I'd rather he was the one who ended it, because of the contract, and because the ten million francs I'll save will ultimately be yours.

Chevalier Forget earthly treasure. Break off with Lélio – make that my ultimate reward.

Countess Please think carefully.

Chevalier You mean you still won't make that sacrifice? Can love really be so limited? How far exactly are you prepared to go for a man like me?

Countess I'll go as far for you as I possibly can.

Chevalier I don't believe you're capable.

Countess I am – I will – I'll send Lélio away – and you can dictate the terms.

Chevalier You'll simply ask him to leave?

Countess Yes.

Chevalier No, my dear Countess, you will not send him away, it's enough that you've agreed to. Your love's unshakeable, and I shan't force you to behave in a way you feel is wrong – certainly not on my account – when my job should be to protect you.

Countess I love you – doesn't that say everything?

Chevalier 'I love you' is all very well – but you must've said the same to Lélio. Don't I deserve more?

Countess Such as?

Chevalier Such as, 'I worship you.' Go on – indulge me – say it.

Countess (The horrible truth is I want to.) You should be ashamed of yourself, asking a woman that.

Chevalier When you've said it, then I'll apologise.

Countess I think he's going to make me.

Chevalier Please – my dearest love – just one short tender phrase. I'm not dangerous – just let the words form in your mouth: would a kiss help?

Countess No – you mustn't – don't you know when to stop? I won't resist you in any way – when the moment comes.

Chevalier The moment's already here – use it – don't be afraid. Shall I help you? Say after me: 'Chevalier, I worship you.'

Countess Chevalier, I worship you.

Chevalier Such music to my ears, my dearest love! One more time.

Countess All right – but don't ask for anything else.

Chevalier Oh? What is it you think I'm going to ask for?

Countess I can't imagine. You go on and on and on. Just stop.

Chevalier Certainly. I'm not without tact, and I would be incapable of damaging any woman's reputation.

Countess I'm marrying you – isn't that enough?

Chevalier I think it's fair to say it's beyond my wildest dreams.

Countess I'm prepared to promise you everlasting fidelity, and happy to lose the ten million francs.

Chevalier But you won't lose anything, if you do what I tell you. Lélio's sure to come and force you to choose between us – make it quite clear that you still agree to marry him. I want you to know what he's like deep down – let me be your guide, and your money's safe – you'll see the man for what he is.

Countess I'll do whatever you say.

SCENE SEVEN

Lélio, Countess, Chevalier.

Lélio Perhaps, Madame, I might interrupt for one moment your conversation with Monsieur. I'm not here to complain so I'll come straight to the point. Not that I couldn't speak at some length if I so wished, given the indifference you've shown since the arrival of Monsieur, whose inadequacy as a man . . .

Chevalier Absolutely.

Lélio I won't go on. My accusations are justified, but clearly unwelcome. I swore to keep my mouth shut – and shut it will stay – whatever the personal cost. I won't ask the obvious questions: why do you detest me? why are you avoiding me? what is it I've done? I'm desperate.

Chevalier laughs.

Oh yes, Monsieur le Chevalier, you may choose to laugh, just as I may choose to wipe that smile off your face.

Chevalier Don't be so angry, Lélio. You said you'd come to the point – straight to the point – but the point is proving somewhat elusive, that's all.

Countess Just control yourself, Lélio, and say what it is you want.

Lélio To know which one of us you intend to choose – Monsieur, or myself. Decide, Madame: the uncertainty is unbearable.

Countess You're upset, Lélio, but understandably so – and I feel for you more than you think. Chevalier, we've had some amusing discussions: now they must end. You've mentioned love – but I'd be cross if I thought you were serious. I'm committed to marry Lélio, just as Lélio is committed to marrying me. Any more complaints?

Lélio None whatsoever – I consider myself privileged – although perhaps / I should add . . .

Countess You don't have to thank me, Lélio, I know how happy this makes you. (The look on his face . . .)

Servant A letter for you, Madame.

Countess Give it here. Would you both excuse me for a moment. It's from my brother.

SCENE EIGHT

Lélio, Chevalier.

Lélio What the hell was all that about? Committed? What exactly is going on?

Chevalier Going on? I've no idea. The whole thing's like a bad dream.

73

Lélio This puts me in a *marvellous* position: I beg her to marry me – she's supposed to say no – then she commits herself. I hope you're not playing games.

Chevalier Me? Play games? What kind of servant do you take me for? One thing might explain it: while we were talking, she started to quiz me about other relationships – I just laughed and brushed it off, but she took it very seriously. That's when you appeared, and she must've acted the way she did simply to punish me. It won't last: I'm the one she loves.

Lélio It makes things extremely difficult.

Chevalier But if she does stay committed, I'd say the only solution is to tell her you'll marry her, but explain you don't love her. Of course you'll have to find a less unpleasant way of putting it. Then point out that if she says no, *she* breaks the contract.

Lélio Sounds pretty crude.

Chevalier Crude? Since when were you so sensitive? What's one more dubious manoeuvre when you stand to gain ten million francs? 'I don't love you, but I would like to marry you. You'd rather not? Then you're breaking our contract. Pay me the money – or pay the price.'

SCENE NINE

Lélio, Countess, Chevalier.

Countess Lélio, my brother can't come till later than I thought. In which case, let's not wait any longer: let's marry as soon as we can.

Chevalier (*under his breath, to Lélio*) One more piece of unpleasantness and it's over.

74

Lélio The thing is, Madame, to be frank with you, I find my feelings have . . . shifted a little.

Countess Shifted? What d'you mean? Have you stopped loving me?

Lélio I wouldn't say exactly stopped – more that some doubts have crept in.

Countess Then just what was that great display of emotion supposed to mean? All that despair – was it just theatre? Because you made it look like a matter of life or death. 'Decide, Madame, the uncertainty is unbearable.'

Lélio The thing is . . . Madame . . . is I assumed there would be no risk, and that you'd turn me down.

Countess Well, what an excellent actor. But where does that leave us with the contract?

Lélio We abide by it, Madame: I would still be delighted to marry you.

Countess What? Marry me when you don't love me?

Lélio A mere detail, Madame: don't let that be any obstacle.

Countess Well, I'm sorry, but I despise you, and absolutely refuse.

Lélio So you'll pay out – yes? – as the contract requires?

Countess I beg your pardon? Where is morality?

Chevalier Don't even ask: I'm afraid this gentleman and morality are totally unacquainted. But why be bound by some degrading contract, when surely the answer – (*producing contract*) – is simply – (*tearing it up*) – to tear it up. (*He laughs.*)

75

Lélio Bastard!

Chevalier (*laughs*) Don't complain, Lélio: you've still got that girl in Paris worth twelve thousand a year. You were told she's beautiful – but I'm afraid they lied – because she's right here – and her face is identical to mine.

Countess Oh my God!

Chevalier I'm not quite the object of desire you thought I was, my dear Countess. And if we'd continued our intimate journey, we might've made some interesting discoveries. Your love has been wasted – true – but your money protected. Later I'll explain exactly how this man intended to trick you.

Countess I don't care what he intended. This trick you've played on me is the cruellest trick imaginable.

Chevalier Cruel? Hardly. If my love turns out to be an illusion, it's an illusion I produced for your own benefit. Look on the pain you're now feeling as a tiny reminder of your own fickleness. Your decision to leave Lélio was not rational, but purely emotional – an error which cannot go entirely unpunished. As for you, Lord Lélio, this is your ring. You gave it me of your own free will, and I give it now in turn to Trivelin and Arlequin. Take it – sell it – and share the money.

Trivelin *and* **Arlequin** Thank you.

Trivelin Here come the musicians.

Chevalier Then stay and listen. I'd hate to think that after all this we had failed to be entertaining.

The musicians play and sing:

SONG: DARK HEART

You say you've been betrayed,
that I have lied and tried to hide the truth
    from you.
You claim the game I've played
altered your mind and was designed to make
    a fool out of you.
One day you'll realise
so-called love was torn apart
by the lies that lie disguised
in your own dark heart.

If I'm not what I seem then face it:
the fact is the act is now over.
Don't hide inside a dream in case it means
you're never going to see the light.
If love becomes unreal don't chase it:
the scene is a simple illusion.
If loving's an ordeal there is no appeal:
accept, forget, don't fight.

You say you've been betrayed,
that I have lied and tried to hide the truth
    from you.
You claim the game I've played
altered your mind and was designed to make
    a fool out of you.
One day you'll realise
so-called love was torn apart
by the lies that lie disguised
in your own dark heart.

Say the play we acted was maybe
destined never to end:
would the words we uttered absurdly

ever be more than pretend?
Love needs love scenes: being in love means
playing the lover's part:
your eyes look into mine, I know that's the sign,
the cue I take from you to start.

You say you've been betrayed,
that I have lied and tried to hide the truth
   from you.
You claim the game I've played
altered your mind and was designed to make
   a fool out of you.
One day you'll realise
so-called love was torn apart
by the lies that lie disguised
in your own dark heart.